Gregg College Keyboarding & Document Processing for Windows™ 8th Edition

Home Lab Version
for Windows 95/98/NT
Internet Ready

User's Guide

Glencoe Customer Software Support

Thank you for purchasing this Glencoe software product. Glencoe is dedicated to providing you with the highest quality software and ensuring that you receive the finest technical support for products you purchase.

To help support our customers, we register all of our software users. To become a registered user, complete the registration card that was included with your software and send it to Glencoe.

Telephone support for all registered users is available between 8 A.M. and 6 P.M. (EST) at 1-800-437-3715. Customers with specific questions can e-mail software support staff at epgtech@mcgraw-hill.com. For basic information or answers to frequently asked questions, visit our Website at www.epgtech.com.

If you have any questions regarding our customer support policy, please e-mail us at the above address or write to us at this address:

Glencoe/McGraw-Hill
ATTN: Software Support Center
8787 Orion Place
Columbus, OH 43240-4027

This document has been prepared with the assistance of Dolphin Inc., Gibbsboro, NJ.

Glencoe/McGraw-Hill

*A Division of The **McGraw-Hill** Companies*

Printed in the United States of America.

P/N G05271.10

2 3 4 5 6 7 8 9 10 054 06 05 04 03 02 01 00

Contents

Program Overview

Gregg College Keyboarding & Document Processing for Windows (GDP) is a Windows-based program designed for use with the *Gregg College Keyboarding & Document Processing for Windows™ 8th Edition* textbook. The software and textbook mirror and reinforce each other. From new key presentations to advanced word processing, all exercises in the textbook are included in one all-encompassing program. For document processing exercises, GDP links to Microsoft Word® 7, 97, or 2000 or Corel WordPerfect® 7 or 8.

Student exercises in GDP are stored on a floppy data disk.

System Requirements

To run GDP, your system must meet the following minimum requirements:

- PC with a 486 (66MHz or higher) or Pentium CPU.
- 16 MB RAM.
- Hard disk with 1 MB of free space.
- High-density 3.5" floppy disk drive (for saving data).
- Graphics adapter, sVGA or higher; 640 x 480; 256-color, True Color, or High Color; small fonts mode.
- Microsoft Windows 95/98/NT.
- Microsoft-compatible mouse and standard keyboard.
- Microsoft Word 7, 97, or 2000 or Corel WordPerfect 7 or 8 for document processing exercises.
- CD-ROM drive.
- A printer is recommended but not required.
- Also recommended: standard audio card compatible with MS Windows MCI.

To use this software for distance learning, your system must also meet the following requirements:

- Modem.
- Windows 95/98/NT MAPI-compatible e-mail program, such as Microsoft Exchange.

GDP supports the following browsers running on a Windows PC: Netscape Navigator 3.0 or 4.0 and Microsoft Internet Explorer 3.0 or 4.0.

Required Text Materials

To complete instructional activities in the program, you will need the following:

- *Gregg College Keyboarding & Document Processing for Windows™ 8th Edition* textbook for the appropriate lessons.
- The GDP manual for the word processing program being used with GDP.
- Student data disk.
- GDP Home Version CD-ROM.

Installing GDP

1. Turn on your computer and start Windows 95/98/NT.
2. Put the GDP Home Version CD-ROM in your CD-ROM drive.
3. Open the Start menu (on the Windows 95/98/NT task bar) and choose *Run....*
4. In the Open blank, type **x:\setup** (where "x:" represents the CD-ROM drive from which you are installing GDP). Click **OK**. See Figure 1-1.

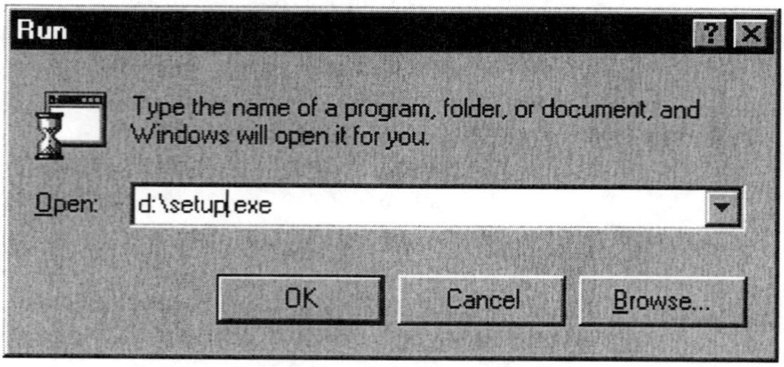

FIGURE 1-1: RUN DIALOG BOX

5. The InstallShield Wizard loads, then the Welcome dialog box displays. Click **Yes** to continue.
6. In the Select Components dialog box, click a button to indicate whether or not you will be using GDP's distance-learning features. Then click **Next**.

- Click **Enable distance-learning features** if you want to be able to use the Internet to send your GDP work files to your instructor and receive information from your instructor.
- Click **Run in standalone mode** if you will not be using the Internet to send your GDP work files to your instructor.

7. In the Choose Destination Location dialog box, select the hard disk and directory where you want to install the software. Click **Browse** to select a location different from the default. If you specify a new directory (that is, one that does not yet exist), the installer notifies you and will create the new directory. After you select a location, click **Next**.
8. In the Student's Data Location Options dialog box, click a button to indicate which floppy disk drive you will use for your GDP data disk. Then click **Next**.
9. The installer now copies files onto your hard disk, a Glencoe Keyboarding program group appears on your desktop, and a final Information dialog box tells you which icon to click to start GDP. Click **OK**.

❖ **Note:** Beginning with Lesson 81, some GDP document processing exercises use the word processor's template files. Check to make sure that the following template files have been installed with your word processor: Memo, Press Release, Purchase Order, Invoice, and all label files. If these templates are not installed, you will be unable to complete GDP exercises that use the templates.

About this User's Guide

The rest of this User's Guide provides the information you need to operate GDP.

- Chapter 2 provides an overview of how GDP works, including detailed instructions for starting the program and logging on, working on GDP exercises, linking to your word processor, viewing and printing your work, and using GDP's distance-learning features.
- Chapter 3 describes GDP's navigational features, including the toolbar, drop-down menus, and keyboard shortcuts.
- Chapter 4 describes the organization of the GDP program and the different types of activities included in the program.
- Appendix A is a troubleshooting guide, which lists common problems and suggested solutions.

- Appendix B summarizes the notation used for error marking and the method used to calculate speed.
- The Index provides a quick way to look up specific information in this User's Guide.

Starting the Program

1. Insert your GDP data disk into the floppy drive and your GDP CD-ROM into the CD-ROM drive.
2. Start Windows 95/98/NT and open the Start menu (on the Windows 95/98/NT task bar).
3. Choose *Programs* and point to *Glencoe Keyboarding*.
4. Select the GDPDL program icon.
5. The opening sequence shows the title and copyright screens. Click anywhere on the title and copyright screens to continue, or wait for the program to sequence through the screens.

Logging on as a Distance-Learning Student

If you have enabled GDP distance-learning features (see step 6 in "Installing GDP" on pages 2-3), your initial log-on sets up the information needed to send your work to your instructor and to receive information from your instructor via the Internet.

1. After you start GDP and go through the opening sequence, the Distance Learning dialog box (Figure 2-1) displays.

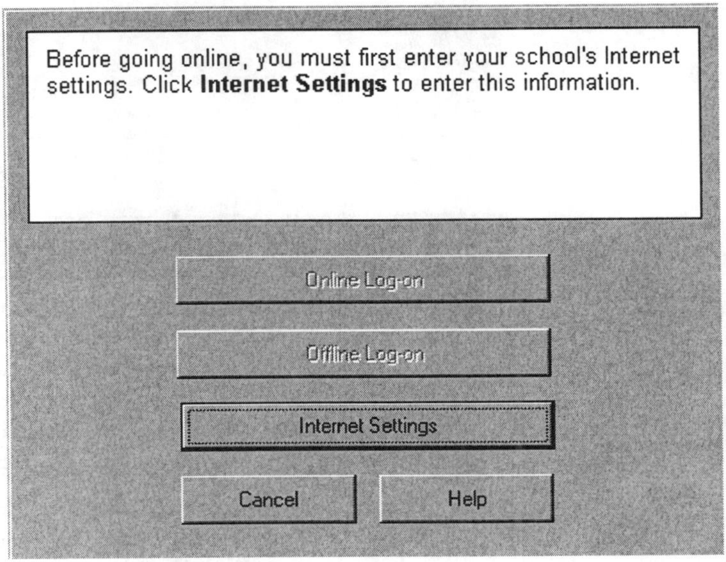

FIGURE 2-1: DISTANCE-LEARNING DIALOG BOX

2. You will need to do an online log-on but, before you do so, you need to specify your Internet settings. Click **Internet Settings**.

3. In the Internet Settings tab of Preferences dialog box (Figure 2-2), type the requested information. This information will tell GDP how to reach that site for uploading your data files and downloading information from your instructor. (Your instructor should be able to provide the FTP information to you.) Click **OK** to save your Internet settings and return to the Distance Learning dialog box.

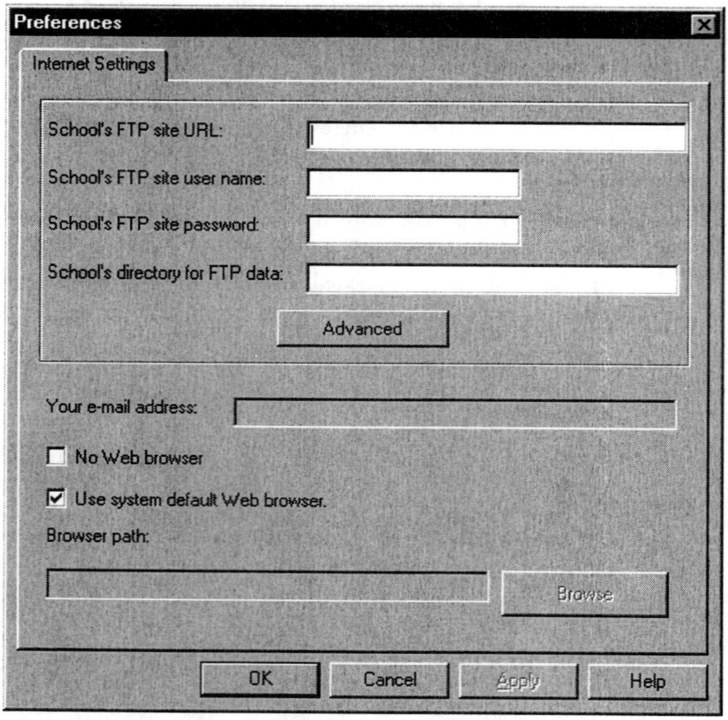

FIGURE 2-2: INTERNET SETTINGS TAB OF PREFERENCES DIALOG BOX

4. Now that GDP knows how to find the school's FTP site, click **Online Log-on** to download log-on information from your instructor. Wait for class files and other information to be downloaded. This may take several minutes.

5. When all necessary information is downloaded to your computer, a Please Note dialog box tells you about the default word processor. Click **OK**. (If your word processor is not

Microsoft Word 2000 or has a path other than C:\Program Files\Microsoft Office\Office\Winword.exe, you will need to change the word processor setting after you log on. See "Setting Preferences," pages 9-10.)

6. The Course/Section List screen displays next. Select your course/section by highlighting its name on the list and clicking **OK**.
7. On the Student List screen, select your name and click **OK**.
8. The Log-on Information screen displays next, with your name and class information already filled in.
   a. In the Options File list box, the EDIT1 options file is selected. To select a different options file, click the down arrow button at the right of the Options File list box and click on (highlight) the name of the desired options file. Be sure to ask your instructor which options file to select. (See the Options Files table on page 9.)
   b. The computer's date appears in the Date field. If the date is incorrect, click on the month, day, or year field and then click the up or down arrow button to adjust the number.

❖ **Note:** The Password field is not required in this version of GDP.

9. Click **Save** to register your log-on information. Several dialog boxes pop up, providing progress information about files that are being checked or transferred to or from the school's FTP site.
10. If your instructor has posted an announcement for your class, it appears on screen, followed by two welcome screens for first-time users and then the Lessons menu, from which you can select a lesson to begin working.

Subsequent Log-ons

When you return to GDP after the initial session, the same Distance Learning dialog box appears, this time giving an additional option to log on offline. Click **Online Log-on** to update information to and from the school's FTP site before beginning work in GDP or **Offline Log-on** to begin working in GDP without first updating information. (While working offline in GDP, you can update files at any time by clicking the **Update Data Through Internet** button on the GDP toolbar.)

Logging on as a Standalone User

If you installed GDP in standalone mode (see step 6 in "Installing GDP" on pages 2-3), your first step is to identify yourself.

1. After you start GDP and go through the opening sequence, a Please Note dialog box tells you about the default word processor. Click **OK**. (If your word processor is not Microsoft Word 2000 or has a path other than C:\Program Files\Microsoft Office\Office\Winword.exe, you will need to change the word processor setting after you log on. See "Setting Preferences," pages 9-10.)
2. The Log-on Information screen (Figure 2-3) displays next. The first time you use GDP, the Log-on Information screen needs to be completed.

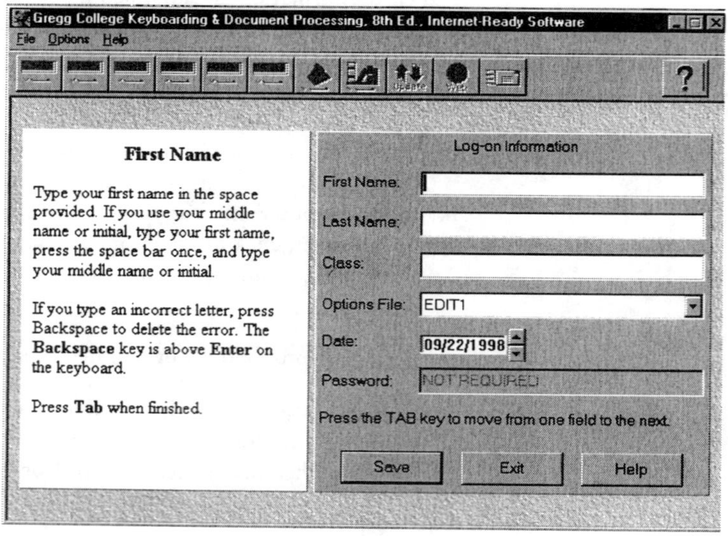

FIGURE 2-3: LOG-ON INFORMATION SCREEN

3. Type your first name, last name, and course/section name, using a mouse click or the **Tab** key to move from one field to the next.
4. In the Options File list box, the EDIT1 options file is selected. To select a different options file, click the down arrow button at the right of the Options File list box and click on (highlight) the name of the desired options file. Be sure to ask your instructor which options file to select. (See the Options Files table on page 9.)
5. The computer's date appears in the Date field. If the date is incorrect, click on the month, day, or year field and then click the up or down arrow button to adjust the number up or down.

❖ **Note:** The Password field is not required in this version of GDP.

6. When finished entering log-on information, click **Save** or press **Enter**.
7. The program records your log-on information for future use, takes you through two welcome screens for first-time users, and then displays the Lessons menu.

Subsequent Log-ons When you return to GDP after logging on initially, you simply check your log-on information, change the Options File or Date field, if necessary, and click **OK** or press **Enter**. The program takes you to the Lessons menu. The exercises folder for the lesson worked on last is open at the bottom of the Lessons menu.

Options Files	
EDIT1*	Editing of timings is allowed, and spacing between sentences is set at 1.
EDIT2	Editing of timings is allowed, and spacing between sentences is set at 2.
NO-EDIT1*	No editing of timings is allowed, and spacing between sentences is set at 1.
NO-EDIT2	No editing of timings is allowed, and spacing between sentences is set at 2.

*Available only when using MS Word 97 or 2000 or Corel WordPerfect 8 as the word processor.

Setting Preferences

During your first session using the Home version of GDP, you need to specify various Internet settings (if you are using GDP's distance-learning features) and your word processor, as follows:

1. Select *Preferences...* on the Options drop-down menu.
2. In the Preferences dialog box, click on the **Internet Settings** or **Word Processor Selection** tab.
3. Specify your settings and click **Apply** to save them. Make changes to the settings on the second tab, if necessary.
4. When you are finished setting preferences, click **OK**.

Internet Settings The Internet Settings tab of the Preferences dialog box is used to specify the location of your school's FTP site, to which GDP will upload your GDP data files and from which GDP will download information from your instructor. This tab is also used to specify your e-mail address and browser location.

FTP information	The fields at the top of the Internet Settings tab are used to specify the following information, which your instructor should have provided to you. School's FTP site URL (unique location on the Internet) School's FTP site user name School's FTP site password School's directory for FTP data (GDP files)
Your e-mail address	Type your full e-mail address in this field. You will need this information in order to be able to receive e-mail from your instructor.
No Web browser	This box should be checked if your computer does not have access to the World Wide Web. If this box is checked, you will not be able to access the school's Website through GDP. (Your school's Website is different than your school's FTP site.)
Use system default Web browser	This box should be checked if you want GDP to use the computer's default Web browser for accessing the school's Website through GDP.
Browser path	If you have access to the World Wide Web but do not want to use your computer's default Web browser, either type the path to the desired browser or click **Browse** and select it in the Find Your Web Browser dialog box.

Word Processor Selection

The Word Processor Selection tab of the Preferences dialog box is used to specify the location of your word processor. Click on the button corresponding to the word processor to be used with GDP. The default path to the selected word processor appears below the list of word processors. If the word processor is in a different location, either type the correct location in the Path box or click **Browse** and select the word processor in the Find Your Word Processor dialog box.

Working on Lesson Exercises

After you log on, the Lessons menu (Figure 2-4) displays a stack of tabbed folders, one for each of the 20 lessons in the current part plus a test to be taken at the end of the part. At the bottom of the screen, a folder displays the exercises for the selected lesson. A black bullet symbol (•) preceding an exercise indicates that the exercise has been completed.

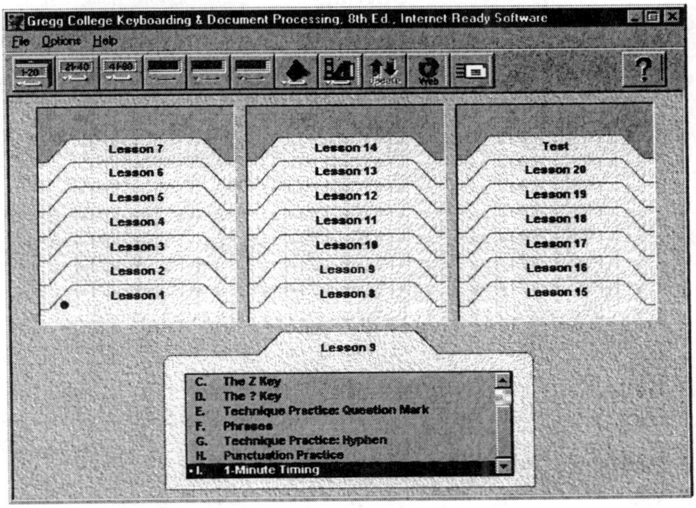

FIGURE 2-4: PART 1 LESSONS MENU

To work on an exercise:

1. Determine if you are viewing the right group of lessons. If not, click on the appropriate Part (file drawer) button on the toolbar.

2. In the top portion of the Lessons menu, click on the folder tab for the lesson on which you want to work. The exercise folder for the selected folder displays at the bottom of the screen.

3. Use the scroll bar to move through the exercise list. Double-click the name of the exercise you want to work on. It is best to begin with the first exercise of a lesson and work through each exercise sequentially.

4. Read the introductory or instruction screen(s) and turn to the appropriate page in the textbook. (For more information about the exercise screen layout, see "The Exercise Screen," page 13.) To continue, click the **Continue** button or press **F6**.

5. Use the toolbar (or shortcut keys) to navigate and to access helpful information:
   - To continue to the next screen or exercise, click the **Continue** button or press **F6**.
   - For general advice on a range of typing topics, click the **Owl Tips** button or press **Ctrl+O**.
   - For formatting instructions for producing different types of documents, click the **Reference Manual** button or press **Ctrl+M**.
   - To access your portfolio, click the **Portfolio** button or press **Ctrl+F**.
   - To return to the previous screen, click the **Previous** button or press **Shift+F6**.
   - To restart a timing within the first 15 seconds, click the **Restart timing** button or press **Ctrl+R**.
   - To exit the exercise and return to the previous menu, click the **Previous Menu** button or press **Esc**.

6. Type the text for the exercise.
   - *Timings*: Type until time is up, at which point the program scores your work and allows you to review the scored text.
   - *Document processing exercises*: Type the document, proofread and use the spelling checker to check your work, and then exit the word processor by selecting *GDP/Return to GDP* on the menu bar.
   - *All other exercises*: Follow on-screen instructions to complete the exercise.

   For more detailed directions, click the **Directions** button on the toolbar.

7. At the end of an exercise, click the **Continue** button or press **F6** to begin the next exercise in the lesson. The program automatically sequences through the exercises in the lesson. At the end of the last exercise for a particular lesson, the program returns to the Lessons menu.

Pressing the **Esc** key allows you to exit an exercise at any time. You can exit the program at any point by selecting *Exit GDP* on the File menu.

The Exercise Screen

Exercise screens have the same basic layout throughout the program (see Figure 2-5):

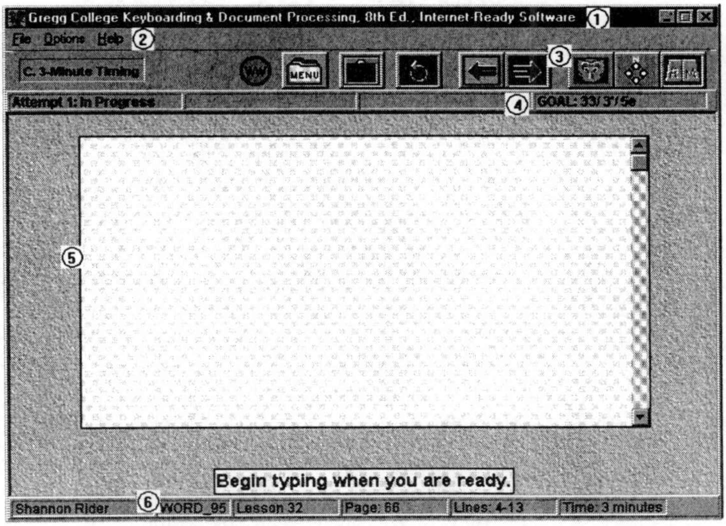

FIGURE 2-5: EXERCISE SCREEN

❶ Title bar: The title bar includes the program name and the standard window control menu box (to the left) and the minimize, maximize, and close buttons (to the right).

❷ Menu bar: The menu bar lists all of the drop-down menus. (See pages 25-27 for more information on specific drop-down menus.)

❸ Toolbar: The toolbar includes the exercise name, the word wrap setting, and icons for navigation and on-screen guidance. (See pages 23-25 for more information on specific icons.)

❹ Dialog bar: The dialog bar specifies information about the current exercise, such as the speed and accuracy goals for a timing and scores on various attempts at the exercise. Goals and scores are noted as follows: number of words/number of minutes/number of errors (for example, "33/3'/5e" indicates 33 words a minute for 3 minutes, with 5 errors).

❺ Body of the screen: The body of the screen provides instructions or an area for typing text.

❻ Status bar: The status bar specifies your name, the options file being used, lesson number, and textbook page. Line numbers and length of a timing are indicated when applicable.

Working on Skillbuilding or Language Arts Exercises

Typically, you should follow the textbook and use the Lessons menu to work on lesson exercises sequentially. Occasionally, you may want to access exercises by type (rather than by lesson), work on special exercises to sharpen keyboarding skills, or focus on particular language arts skills for a session. In such cases, use the Skillbuilding or Language Arts menus to access exercises.

- The Skillbuilding menu groups exercises by type and includes all exercises except for tests, language arts exercises, and document processing exercises. The Skillbuilding menu also includes Open Timings, Custom Timings, Supplementary Timings, Numeric Keypad Practice, and the Tennis Game, which are not included in lesson exercises. To access the Skillbuilding menu, click the **Skillbuilding Exercises** button on the toolbar.
- The Language Arts menu includes all of the language arts exercises (including several interactive tutorials) and groups them by skill area. To access the Language Arts menu, click the **Language Arts** button on the toolbar.

The exercises accessible on the Skillbuilding and Language Arts menus work exactly the same as the corresponding exercises in the Lessons menu. For questions about how a particular exercise works, click the **Directions** button on the toolbar.

Linking to the Word Processor Outside of an Exercise

For documents that are included in the textbook exercises, GDP automatically links to the word processor specified in your Preferences (see "Setting Preferences," pages 9-10). The *Go to Word Processor* option on the File drop-down menu is for working on other documents not included in the textbook or for printing a formatted GDP document without having to access the document through the Lessons menu.

To link to the word processor outside of a textbook exercise:

1. From a menu screen, select *Go to Word Processor* on the File menu.
2. The word processor opens a new document window. You can type a new document in the blank window or open an existing document by selecting *Open* on the File menu.
3. When finished working on the document, select *Return to GDP* on the GDP menu on the word processor's menu bar.

STOP ALERT: The GDP program adds the GDP menu to the word processor's menu bar to provide you an easy, seamless route back to GDP and ensure that documents created outside of GDP exercises are saved to your data disk. Make sure that you use this method to exit the word processor.

❖ Note: If a document is included in the GDP program, that document will be located on your data disk. GDP document file names follow these conventions: a letter-number code corresponding the type and number of the document followed by a period and the extension assigned by the word processor. For example, the full file name for Memo 15 is "M15.DOC" in MS Word and "M15.WPD" in WordPerfect.

Viewing and Printing Your Work

GDP provides a chart and two types of reports to help you keep track of your progress and review completed exercises. The chart and reports can be viewed on screen and printed.

Portfolio Your Portfolio contains two types of reports. The Summary Report provides a single line of information for all exercises on which you have worked, with results and completion status for each. Detailed Reports include the scored text for any exercise on which you have worked—unless you have used the *Delete Files* option on the File drop-down menu to delete some exercises.

To access your reports:

1. Click the **Portfolio** button on the toolbar or select the *Portfolio...* option on the File drop-down menu. The Portfolio Options dialog box (Figure 2-6) displays.

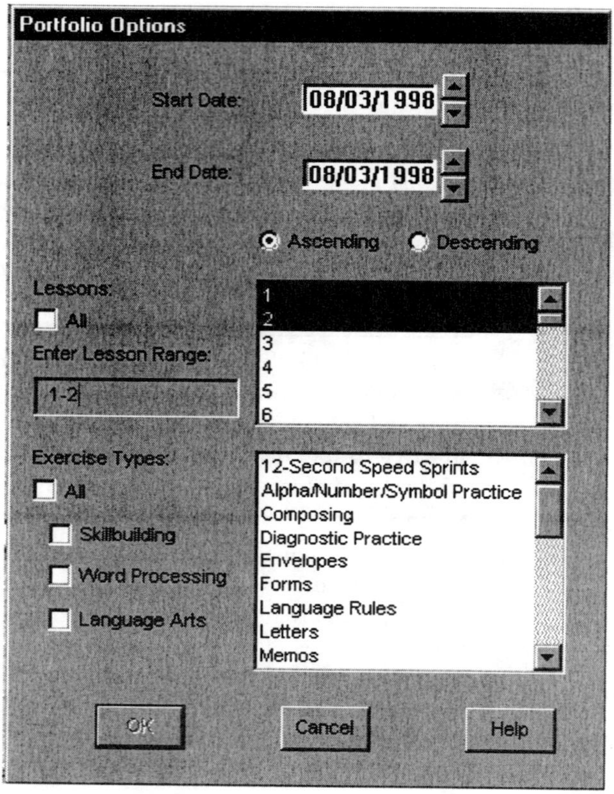

FIGURE 2-6: PORTFOLIO OPTIONS DIALOG BOX

2. Specify a date range, sort order (ascending or descending by date), lesson(s), and exercise type(s) to include in the Summary Report, and then click **OK** or press **Enter**.

❖ **Note:** At least one lesson number and at least one exercise type must be specified in order for a Summary Report to be generated.

3. The Summary Report window (Figure 2-7) lists all of the completed exercises specified for Portfolio Options, one exercise per line.

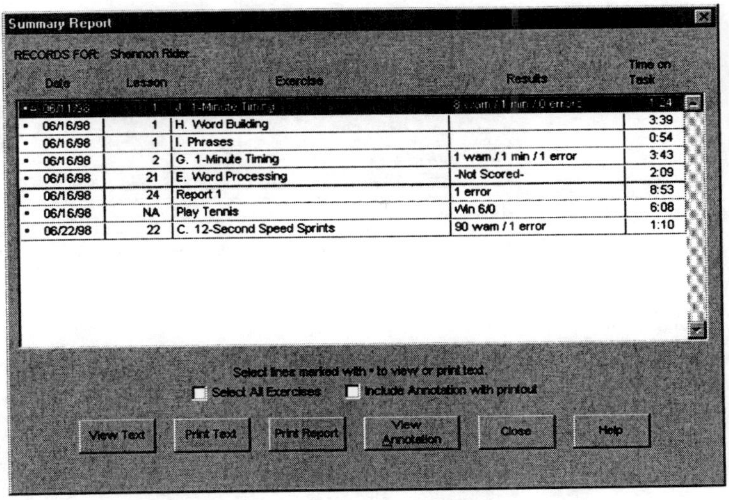

FIGURE 2-7: SUMMARY REPORT WINDOW

For each exercise, the Summary Report lists:

- Completion date
- Lesson number, exercise letter, and exercise description
- Results: WAM speed and number of errors for scored exercises; blank for unscored exercises
- Time on Task: total elapsed time in the exercise beginning with the first instruction screen

4. To print a copy of the Summary Report, click **Print Report**. To print a copy of the scored text for any exercise, click once on the lines for the desired exercises (they must be preceded by a black bullet in the Date column) and then click **Print Text**.

5. If your instructor has written comments (an annotation) about your performance on an exercise, an "A" appears preceding the date in the Date column. To view your instructor's comments, click once on the exercise line and then click **View Annotation**. In the Annotations dialog box, click **Print** to print a copy of your comments or **Done** to return to the Summary Report.

6. To view the text for any exercises (that is, get a Detailed Report), click on the desired exercise lines on the Summary Report (they must be preceded by a black bullet in the Date column) and click **View Text**. The Detailed Report window (Figure 2-8) displays your text and scores.

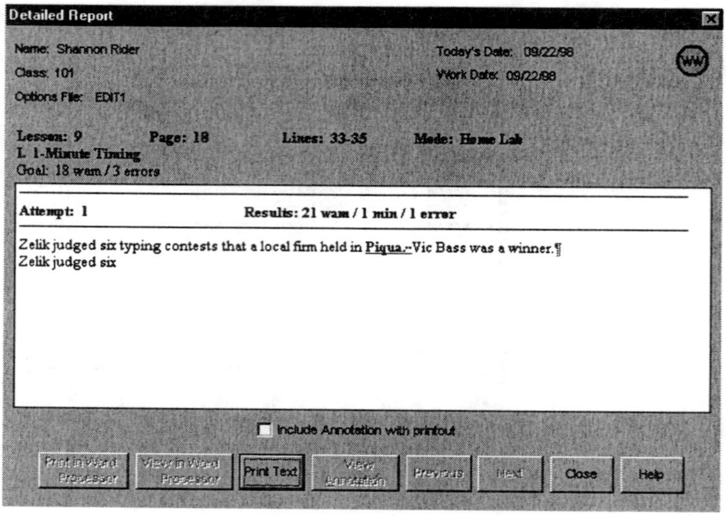

FIGURE 2-8: DETAILED REPORT WINDOW

- To print the Detailed Report, click **Print Text**.
- If you selected more than one exercise, **Next** and **Previous** buttons can be used to move among the Detailed Reports.
- Documents appear as unformatted, scored text. To view the formatted document as it appears in the word processor, click **View in Word Processor**. You will be able to make changes to the document, but those changes will not be saved. To return to GDP, select *Return to GDP* on the GDP menu on the menu bar.
- To print a formatted version of the document (without viewing it in the word processor), click **Print in Word Processor**.
- When finished viewing the Detailed Reports, click **Close** to return to the Summary Report.

7. To exit the Summary Report, click **Close**. To close the Portfolio Options dialog box, click **Cancel**.

The Performance Chart

The Performance Chart shows graphically how your speed and accuracy scores on timings have changed from the beginning of a part to the end of that part (a group of 20 lessons).

To view the Performance Chart, select *Performance Chart* on the File drop-down menu. The Performance Chart window (Figure 2-9) is a bar graph that plots your speed and errors for each timing in the part. Speed appears in yellow and errors appear in red. The speed goal and error tolerance for the timing are marked as horizontal lines on each timing bar. A yellow smiley face appears above each timing for which you met both speed and accuracy goals.

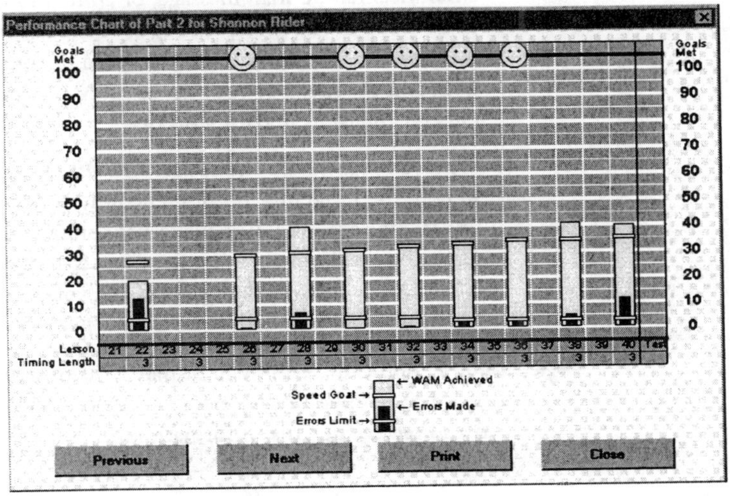

FIGURE 2-9: PERFORMANCE CHART

- To print a copy of the Performance Chart for the current part, click **Print**.
- To view the Performance Chart for the previous part (the part number appears in the title bar of the window), click **Previous**. To view the Performance Chart for the next part, click **Next**.
- To close the Performance Chart, click **Close**.

Updating Data Through the Internet

If you are using GDP's distance-learning features, you need to update data files periodically—that is, send your work to your instructor and receive information from your instructor. When starting GDP, you can do an Online Log-on to update data. In addition, you can update data files at any time during a GDP session by following this procedure:

1. Click the **Update Data Through Internet** button on the toolbar. The Internet File Update dialog box appears.
2. To update only files that have changed since the last update through the Internet, click **Update New**. To update all files, regardless of when they were updated, click **Update All**. (**Update All** will take longer than **Update New**.)

3. At this point, GDP establishes an online connection to the school's FTP site, uploads your files to the school's FTP site, and downloads information from your instructor (for example, an announcement, e-mail message, or annotation). This process can take several minutes, depending on the amount of information that needs to be transmitted, the speed of your Internet connection, and the speed of your modem. Messages (with progress meters) appear as updating occurs.
4. When all files have been updated, GDP returns to where you were in the program. If GDP encounters a problem during the update (for example, if the Internet connection went down), a dialog box will indicate that the transfer failed or was aborted. Click **OK** to proceed, and then check your Internet settings and try again. (See "Setting Preferences," pages 9-10.)

❖ **Note:** Periodically, GDP will display a dialog box reminding you to update data. When this happens, you should click **Update Files** to send and receive updated information.

Sending E-mail to Your Instructor

If your instructor has assigned himself or herself an e-mail address for you to use in GDP, you can send your instructor e-mail messages through GDP. In order for the e-mail feature to work properly in GDP, your e-mail system must be MAPI-compliant (most Windows 95/98/NT e-mail systems are MAPI-compliant). To send an e-mail message to your instructor from within GDP:

1. Select *E-mail Instructor...* on the File drop-down menu or click the **E-mail Instructor** button on the toolbar.

❖ **Note:** If you do not have a MAPI-compliant e-mail system, a Choose Profile dialog box appears at this point. You can now set up Microsoft Exchange for use as your GDP e-mail system. (Doing so will not disable other e-mail systems installed on your system.) Otherwise, click **Cancel**. Two messages will appear, the first indicating that you canceled and the second providing your instructor's e-mail address in case you want to e-mail your instructor from outside of GDP.

2. An addressed e-mail message window appears. Type a subject and a message.
3. When ready to send the message, click the **Send** button.

Accessing Your School's Website

You can access your school's Website through GDP if you have access to the World Wide Web (Web) and if your instructor has set up your class for access to your school's Website.

To access the school's Website from GDP:

1. Click the **Access Campus Website** button on the toolbar.
2. GDP launches your browser, which establishes an online connection and displays the school's Website home page.
3. When finished browsing the school's Website, you can either close the browser window or switch back to GDP using the Windows 95/98/NT task bar.

❖ **Note:** Check your browser setting before trying to access the school's Website. (See "Setting Preferences," pages 9-10.)

To navigate in GDP, use the toolbar, drop-down menus, and/or keyboard shortcuts.

Toolbar

The toolbar is a row of buttons running across the top of the screen just below the menu bar. Use the buttons on the toolbar to move around within GDP. When you rest the mouse pointer over a button on the toolbar, a Tooltip shows the name of the button and the keyboard shortcut, if there is one. See "Keyboard Shortcuts," page 27.

Toolbar on Menu Screens

Part buttons
Use these buttons (which look like file drawers) to go to the Lessons menu for a particular part or group of 20 lessons. The Lessons menu displays all of the lessons and exercises in the part.

Skillbuilding Exercises button
Use this button to go to the Skillbuilding menu, which groups exercises by type and includes all of the lesson exercises except for tests, language arts exercises, and document processing exercises. The Skillbuilding menu also includes Open Timings, Custom Timings, Supplementary Timings, Numeric Keypad Practice, and the Tennis Game, which are not accessible from Lessons menus.

Language Arts button
Use this button to go to the Language Arts menu, which displays all of the language arts exercises in the program. The Language Arts menu provides access to language arts exercises by skill area (rather than by lesson) and includes numerous interactive language arts tutorials not found in the textbook.

Update Data Through Internet button
Use this button if you are a distance-learning student and you want to send your GDP files to your school's FTP site or receive information from your instructor via your

school's FTP site. For more information, see "Updating Data Through the Internet," pages 19-20.

Access Campus Website button
Use this button to access your school's Website. This button is active only if you have access to the Web and your instructor has set up Internet access for you. For more information, see "Accessing Your School's Website," page 21.

E-mail Instructor button
Use this button to create and send an e-mail message to your instructor (if your instructor has assigned himself or herself an e-mail address). For more information, see "Sending E-mail to Your Instructor," page xx.

Help button
Use this button to get information about how GDP works.

Toolbar on Exercise Screens

Previous Menu button
Use this button to return to the previous menu.

Portfolio button
Use this button to access student reports.

Restart timing button
Use this button to restart a timing within the first 15 seconds. This feature is very helpful if you realize that you made a mistake right at the beginning of the timing—such as having Caps Lock on, forgetting to tab, or forgetting to capitalize the first word.

Previous button
Use this button to move back to the previous screen in the exercise.

Continue button
Use this button to move on to the next screen in the exercise.

Owl Tips button
Use this button to get general typing tips.

Directions button
Use this button to get directions for completing the current exercise.

Reference Manual button
Use this button for help with formatting the various types of documents included in GDP.

Drop-Down Menus

Drop-down menus can be accessed using a mouse or the keyboard.

- Mouse: click on a menu bar item to display its drop-down menu, and then click on the desired option.
- Keyboard: press the **Alt** key to activate the menu bar, type the underlined letter of the desired menu, use the down arrow key to move to the desired option, and then press **Enter**.

To deactivate the menu bar, press **Alt** or click anywhere on the screen other than on the menu bar or in a drop-down menu.

File Menu

Portfolio...
Use *Portfolio...* to view or print a report showing your scores on completed GDP exercises as well as scored text for any exercise. The report can be restricted by date range, lesson number, or exercise type.

Performance Chart...
Use *Performance Chart...* to view or print a graph showing your speed and accuracy on all timings in a part.

Go to Word Processor
Use *Go to Word Processor* to link to your word processing program to work on documents that are not included in the textbook or to print copies of completed documents without accessing those documents through the lesson's exercise folder. For more information, see "Linking to the Word Processor Outside of an Exercise," page 14.

Show Announcement
Use *Show Announcement* to view an announcement that your instructor has sent to your class. If your instructor has not posted an announcement for your class, this option is inactive.

E-mail Instructor...
Use *E-mail Instructor...* to create and send an e-mail message to your instructor, if your instructor has assigned himself or herself an e-mail address. For more information, see "Sending E-mail to Your Instructor," page 20.

Delete Files
Use *Delete Files* to delete your text for selected exercise types. For a selected unit or group of units, you can delete document processing exercises and/or language arts and skillbuilding exercises.

❖ **Note:** When *Delete Files* is used, only the scored text is deleted. Scores are maintained in your Portfolio, but the bullet preceding the date in the Summary Report is removed (indicating that a Detailed Report is not available).

Exit GDP
Use *Exit GDP* to exit the program.

Options Menu

Personal Information...
Personal Information is used to enter information such as initials, a byline, and your instructor's name. GDP opens the Personal Information form when you need to add information.

Preferences...
Preferences... is used to specify your Internet settings (if you are using GDP's distance-learning features) and the word processor that will be used in document processing exercises. See "Setting Preferences," pages 9-10.

Instructor Options
Instructor Options is inactive in this version of GDP.

Help Menu

Program Overview
Use *Program Overview* for a quick introduction to GDP.

Reference Manual
Use *Reference Manual* for detailed instructions on formatting the various types of documents produced in GDP.

Help
Use *Help* to view the contents tab for Help topics.

About...
Use *About...* to determine which version of the program is being used. This information is useful when calling customer support.

Keyboard Shortcuts

Sometimes it is easier to use a keyboard shortcut rather than to remove your hand from the keyboard to activate the mouse. Here are the keyboard shortcuts in GDP:

Alt	**Menu bar** Activates the menu bar.
Alt+F4	**Exit** Exits the program. Not active within an exercise (press **Esc** to cancel the exercise first).
Ctrl+D	**Directions** Provides directions for working on the current exercise.
Ctrl+M	**Reference Manual** Provides formatting guidelines for various types of documents.
Ctrl+O	**Owl Tips** Provides general tips on a range of topics related to typing.
Ctrl+F	**Portfolio** Accesses student reports.
Ctrl+R	**Restart timing** Allows you to restart most timings within the first 15 seconds.
Esc	**Previous Menu** Cancels an exercise. If a scored exercise, the report is marked canceled.
F1	**Help** Opens Help.
F6	**Continue** Moves to the next screen in an exercise.
Shift+F6	**Previous** Moves back to the previous screen in an exercise.

Organization

The basic organization of GDP matches that of the textbook. Exercises are presented in lessons, and 20 lessons comprise a part. Each lesson is designed to be completed in a 55- to 60-minute period. To go through the program sequentially from one lesson to the next, use the Lessons menu. It is recommended that you complete all of the lesson's exercises and in sequence. As each exercise is completed, GDP automatically moves to the next exercise in the lesson. To get out of this automatic sequence and return to the Lessons menu, click the **Previous Menu** button or press the **Esc** key.

Two other menus in GDP allow you to access exercises outside of the lesson structure. The Skillbuilding menu groups exercises by type and also includes several types of exercises not covered in the lesson exercises. These exercises are all designed to build keyboarding skills. The Language Arts menu groups all of the program's language arts exercises by skill area, allowing you to focus on particular language arts problem areas.

Lessons Menu

Each Lessons menu consists of a stack of 20 tabbed folders, one folder per lesson. To access the Lessons menu for a given part, click one of the **Part** buttons on the toolbar (each button specifies the lesson range).

Skillbuilding Menu

The Skillbuilding menu includes all drills, timings, and practices from lesson exercises, plus the following: Open Timings, Custom Timings, Supplementary Timings, Numeric Keypad Practice, and the Tennis Game. To access the Skillbuilding menu, click the **Skillbuilding Exercises** button on the toolbar.

Language Arts Menu

The Language Arts menu includes all of the language arts exercises included in the textbook, plus numerous interactive language arts tutorials. The Language Arts menu groups exercises into the following skill areas: abbreviations, adjectives/adverbs, agreement, apostrophe, capitalization, comma, composing, hyphen, number expression, other punctuation, pronouns, proofreading, quotation marks, italics, spelling, and word usage. To access the Language Arts menu, click the **Language Arts** button on the toolbar.

Types of Exercises

The exercises in GDP parallel those in the textbook. The software can time, score, repeat an exercise, diagnose (and recommend corrective practice), deliver instruction, and provide directions for the exercises. The major types of exercises are described briefly in this section. For specific directions for a particular exercise, click the **Directions** button on the toolbar.

Document Processing

GDP links to your word processor for document processing exercises. That link is specified in your Preferences (see "Setting Preferences," pages 9-10).

Documents in the Textbook

To produce a document in the textbook, select the document from the lesson's exercise folder on the Lessons menu. The Document Options dialog box displays your options for the file to be used for the exercise. Choose an option, and GDP links to the word processor.

❖ **Note:** The Document Options dialog box does not appear for practice exercises done in the word processing manual.

Unless otherwise instructed, use the default settings of the word processor. Type the document, proofread it, and spell-check it.

When finished working on the document, exit the word processor by selecting *Return to GDP* on the menu bar. A dialog box asks if you want to save the file; you must click **Yes** in order for the document to be saved. If this is a scored exercise, the next dialog box asks if you want the document scored. If the document is incomplete, you should click **No**. If it is complete, clicking **Yes** will score the document and give you an opportunity to review the scored text.

Documents are scored for keystrokes only, not for formatting. You may want to print a document. If you print the document within the word processor (before returning to GDP), exercise time on task accumulates while the document is printing, and the document prints without a header (your name, class, and date information). Another printing method, which includes a header and does not add time to the exercise, is to print the document from your Portfolio. To do so, access the Portfolio (from the File drop-down menu or the toolbar), select the document on the Summary Report, click **View Text**, and then click **Print in Word Processor**.

STOP ALERT: In order for GDP to score mail-merge documents, labels, and templates correctly, the files must be saved with a specific file name. A reminder is provided, as well as the specific file name, in the Document Options dialog box. Special directions are provided for mail merge exercises in Help (select *Help* on the Help menu), in the "How to" section of the Contents tab.

Documents Not in the Textbook To create documents NOT in the textbook, you can link to the word processor by selecting *Go to Word Processor* from the File drop-down menu.

When documents are prepared this way, you will have to create a name for and save the document. It is recommended that you use a separate data disk for documents not included in the textbook.

For more information, see "Linking to the Word Processor Outside of an Exercise," page 14.

Language Arts These exercises are designed to help you improve language skills for business. Typically, a language arts exercise introduces a rule and illustrates its use by giving examples. Then GDP tests your understanding of the rule by asking you to apply it in a particular passage. Each language rule that is presented in the textbook can be reviewed by using the interactive "Rule" tutorial found in the software.

Language arts exercises can be accessed through the Lessons menu or through the Language Arts menu. When accessed through the Language Arts menu, the exercises are organized by skill area. Select a skill area folder, and all exercises for that skill area are listed in the open folder at the bottom of the menu. Exercises that are covered in the textbook appear with their lesson number and exercise letter; the special tutorials are designated as "Rule:" exercises.

New Key Drills New key drills introduce you to new keyboard characters. GDP tells you which finger to use and offers a demonstration of correct keyboarding for the character. As you progress through the exercise, you will type several lock-stepped sequences of the new keys, which require that the correct key be typed before continuing. After each lock-stepped line, there are additional drill lines for you to type.

Other Drills Drills other than new key exercises generally focus on either speed or accuracy.

Accuracy Pattern

Each group of practice lines is typed twice:

```
jamb lamb limb limp lump bump pump jump
pals pale sale same sane vane cane cape
cure core cove wove move more mare maze

jamb lamb limb limp lump bump pump jump
pals pale sale same sane vane cane cape
cure core cove wove move more mare maze
```

Speed Pattern

Each practice line is typed twice before proceeding to the next line:

```
jamb lamb limb limp lump bump pump jump
jamb lamb limb limp lump bump pump jump

pals pale sale same sane vane cane cape
pals pale sale same sane vane cane cape

cure core cove wove move more mare maze
cure core cove wove move more mare maze
```

Numeric Keypad

The numeric keypad exercises, which are accessible from the Skillbuilding menu only, teach you how to use the numeric keypad and build skills in typing numbers. There are three sections of numeric keypad exercises:

- **Introduction** exercises teach the keys on the numeric keypad. They are very similar to new key drills on the standard keyboard.
- **Pretest/practice/posttest** sequences resemble other pretest/practice/posttest sequences, except that you type numbers in right-justified columns rather than text in a blank input screen.
- **Practice** exercises are additional, scored exercises that focus on particular kinds of numbers (e.g., long decimal numbers).

The timing and scoring of numeric keypad exercises differs from those of text-based exercises. Time in numeric keypad exercises is recorded as the number of seconds it takes you to complete the exercise (e.g., S 193 means that you took 193 seconds to complete the exercise). Speed in numeric keypad exercises is reported in digits per minute (e.g., 101 DPM).

❖ **Note:** On screen, numbers with four or more digits appear with commas to make reading easier. You should not type the comma.

Tennis Game

The tennis game is an interactive game designed to help you improve speed, accuracy, and concentration on the keyboard. The tennis game is accessible from the Skillbuilding menu. Results from completed matches are saved by GDP and appear in your Portfolio.

To play the tennis game:

1. Select the Tennis Game folder on the Skillbuilding menu, then select the Tennis Game exercise in the open folder.
2. After reading the introductory mouse screen, click the **Continue** button.
3. On the Game Options screen (Figure 4-1), select the following:
   - *Skill Level,* from 1 to 5. The skill level determines the speed of play, with 5 being the fastest speed. To lower or raise the level, click the left-arrow or right-arrow button on the Select a Skill Level panel. Your opponent's name is determined by the skill level chosen (e.g., Novice for level 1).
   - *Number of Sets,* 1 or 3. A tennis match can consist of one or three sets, each set consisting of six games. Click either the **1 Set** button or the **3 Sets** button in the Select the Number of Sets panel.
   - *Sound,* on or off. You can choose to play the game with or without sound by clicking the Sound **on** or **off** radio button. If the game is played with sound, score results, audience reactions, and ball bounces are audible.
   - *Game Keys,* by all keys, by row, by finger, by learned keys, or individually selected. You have these choices: to select all keys learned so far in GDP New Key Drills (the default, shown with red dots on the on-screen keyboard), click **Select Learned Keys**; to select all keys on the keyboard, click **Select All Keys**; to select all keys in a particular row of the keyboard, click the arrow button to the right of the corresponding row on the on-screen keyboard; to select all keys for a particular finger, click a finger in the Select by Fingers area; to select keys individually, click the desired keys on the on-screen keyboard. Selected keys are shown in light green on the on-screen keyboard. To clear all keys and begin selecting game keys from scratch, click **Clear All Keys**. To deselect a choice, click the selection button again.

- *Game Demo.* Check this option to see the tennis game operate by itself. Once the option is checked, click the **Continue** button to see the game played in Demo mode. Demo mode uses the current set of game options (e.g., number of sets and skill level). To return to the Game Options screen, click the **Previous** button.

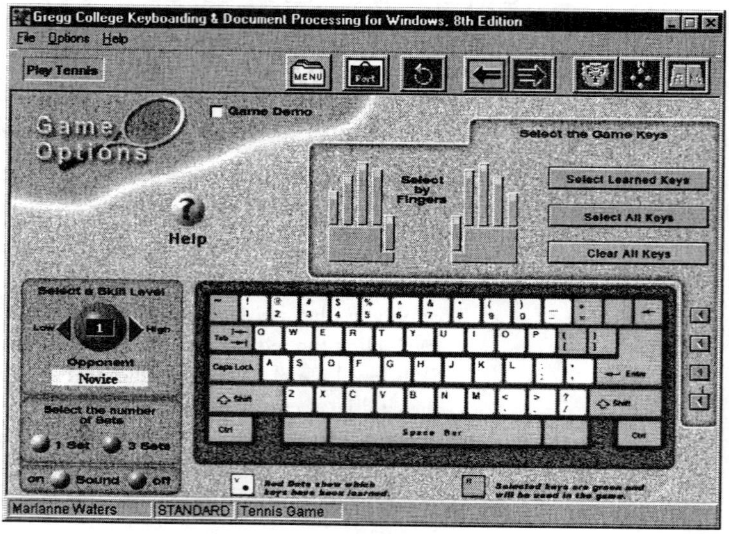

FIGURE 4-1: GAME OPTIONS SCREEN

4. To begin playing the game, click the **Continue** button.
5. Two players appear on the play screen (Figure 4-2). You are in the left court and your opponent is in the right court. The scoreboard appears at the top of the screen. To begin the game and serve the ball, press **Enter**.

FIGURE 4-2: PLAY SCREEN

6. The ball is served to your opponent's court. When your opponent returns the serve, a keyboard character appears in a white box covering part of the net. The object is for you to type that character as fast as possible.
   - If you type the correct character before the ball crosses the net, you win the point.
   - If you type the correct character after the ball crosses the net but before the ball reaches you, no point is scored and the rally continues.
   - If you type the wrong character or type the correct character but after the ball reaches you, your opponent wins the point.

❖ **Note:** Scoring follows standard tennis rules. A game is won by the first person to win 4 points (15, 30, 40, game), but must be won by at least two points. The score for a game tied at 40 to 40 is called "deuce," and the score for a player who has one point more than the other player (above 40) is called "advantage." A set is won by the first person to win 6 games, but must be won by at least two games. At any time during a match, you can review the rules of the game by clicking the **Rules** button in the bottom right-hand corner of the play screen.

7. After each point, press **Enter** to serve for the next point. At the end of a game, the scoreboard is updated and the next game begins. At the end of the match (i.e., after either 1 or 3 sets), the winner is announced, your scores are recorded in the Portfolio, and the program asks if you want a rematch.

At any time during a match, you can exit. If the match is incomplete, GDP does not save your results.

Tests The timing tests and the document processing tests for each part of the textbook appear in the software as the Test folder in the Lessons menu for the part. The part tests are included in the textbook. The material for the alternate part tests is in the *Instructor's Manual.* When you are ready to take an alternate part test, be sure to get the material for the text from your instructor.

The results of the timing tests will be recorded in the Summary Report and the copy will be treated like any other completed exercise. Document processing tests are scored for keystrokes only. Be sure to print a copy of these documents to submit to your instructor.

Timings There are several types of timings in GDP, including 1- to 5-minute timings in lesson exercises (accessible from the Lessons menu) plus additional Open, Custom, and Supplementary timings (accessible from the Skillbuilding menu only). All types of timings work essentially the same:

1. Select the timing from the lesson exercise folder on the Lessons menu or from one of the timings folders on the Skillbuilding menu. In some cases, you are allowed to choose the timing duration.

2. After reading the introductory/instruction screens, turn to the appropriate passage in the textbook and click the **Continue** button to begin the timing. (For Custom Timings, get the material for the text from your instructor. Any text can be used for Open Timings; Open Timings are scored for speed only.)

3. Type the copy and, if finished typing the passage before time is up, press **Enter** and begin typing the passage again. Depending on the options file you are using, the **Backspace**, cursor movement, and **Delete** keys may or may not be enabled (see the Options Files table on page 9).

❖ **Note:** For timings that allow you to restart during the first 15 seconds, a beep indicates when the restart period is over. For 3- and 5-minute timings, a beep signals when 30 seconds remain. For all timings, a beep signals when time is up.

4. When time is up, the copy is scored for both speed and accuracy (except for Open Timings, which are scored for speed only). Your scores will display at the top of the screen.
5. Review the scored copy to pinpoint errors.
6. If desired, you can repeat the timing.

❖ **Note:** For information on the formula used to calculate speed or the way errors are marked in scored copy, see Appendix B.

Appendix A: Troubleshooting Guide

If you have any questions or problems as you install or run GDP, first make sure that your system meets the requirements outlined in "System Requirements," page 1, and that you followed the exact procedure outlined in "Installing GDP," pages 2-3. Next, check this troubleshooting guide. If you experience a problem not covered here or not remedied by following a suggestion listed here, record exactly at what point in the program the problem occurred and a description of what happened when you encountered the problem. Then call Glencoe's customer software support center at **1-800-437-3715** (8 A.M. - 6 P.M. EST).

❖ **Note:** If you suspect that you have a defective disk, do not modify it in any way. Glencoe will not be responsible for disks that have been recopied, reformatted, or purchased from a source other than Glencoe.

■ **When installing GDP, the Choose Destination Location dialog box indicates that the drive does not have sufficient free space.**

Explanation: GDP requires 1 MB of free hard-disk space, which the selected drive does not have.

Suggestion: If you have another hard disk drive with at least 1 MB of free space, select that other drive and click **OK** to continue the GDP installation. Otherwise, press **Esc** to cancel the installation, then free up at least 1 MB of space on your hard disk and run the GDP installation again.

■ **When starting the program, a dialog box prompts you to insert a data disk.**

Explanation 1: There is no data disk in the floppy drive.

Suggestion: Insert the data disk in the floppy drive specified in parentheses after the GDPDL program icon name.

Explanation 2: The data disk is defective.

Suggestion: Inform your instructor.

■ **You are a distance-learning student and get a message "Error downloading your class information from the Internet. Verify your Internet settings and try again or contact your instructor" or "Internet file transfer failed or aborted. Verify your Internet settings and try again or contact your instructor."**

Explanation 1: Your FTP settings are incorrect. It is also possible that your school's FTP site is case-sensitive and your settings do not match the case required by the FTP site.

Suggestion: Ask your instructor for precise information about your school's FTP settings. Then launch GDP and access Internet Settings. In the Internet Settings dialog box, enter your school's FTP site URL, user name, and password, as well as the school's directory for FTP data. Use the same capitalization that was provided by your instructor.

Explanation 2: These messages also appear if the link between your computer and your school's FTP site is not functioning properly, if the link between your Internet service provider is not functioning properly, or if the transmission is interrupted.

Suggestion: Establish a new connection with your Internet service provider to ensure that the link and the service provider are functioning. If you still encounter the error message, inform your instructor.

- **A message indicates that the data disk is full.**

Explanation: You are about to exceed the available disk space on the data disk and need to free disk space before continuing.

Suggestion: When this message appears, click **OK** to close the message dialog box. Exit GDP and make a copy of the full data disk, if you wish. Then restart GDP, log on, and select *Delete Files* on the File drop-down menu. In the Delete Files dialog box, select the unit(s) and exercise types to delete and click **OK**. In the Confirm dialog box, click **Yes** or **Yes to All** to delete the selected files. When you delete files, you delete text (Detailed Reports) only. Scores for exercises with deleted text are retained on the Summary Report.

- **A message indicates that the Summary Report file is full.**

Explanation: The maximum number of exercises that can be listed on a Summary Report is 500. When the Summary Report exceeds 500 exercises, the program automatically overwrites exercises starting with the oldest first. When this happens, you will not be able to access old exercises that are overwritten on the Summary Report.

Suggestion: Make a copy of the data disk (or data directory), to have in case you want to access old exercises that will not be accessible when GDP is used in the future. Then continue using GDP.

- **A message indicates that the maximum number of Detailed Reports has been reached.**

  Explanation: The maximum number of Detailed Reports that can be accessible from a Summary Report is 200. When the maximum is reached, the program makes room for new Detailed Reports by deleting Detailed Reports, starting with the oldest first. When this happens, you will not be able to access Detailed Reports for the exercises that are deleted.

  Suggestion: Exit GDP and make a copy of the full data disk if you wish. Then restart GDP, log on, and select *Delete Files* on the File drop-down menu. In the Delete Files dialog box, select the unit(s) and exercise types to delete and click **OK**. In the Confirm dialog box, click **Yes** or **Yes to All** to delete the selected files. When you delete files, you delete text (Detailed Reports) only. Scores for exercises with deleted text are retained on the Summary Report.

- **For document processing exercises, GDP fails to start the word processor.**

  Explanation: The word processor's location specified in your Preferences is incorrect or is the location for a different version of the word processor.

  Suggestion: Select *Preferences...* on the Options drop-down menu, select the Word Processor tab, and then change the selected word processor or path. See "Setting Preferences," pages 9-10.

- **When accessing a document processing exercise, GDP indicates that it cannot find the required word processor template file.**

  Explanation: A word processor template file that GDP uses for the selected exercise is not installed on your system.

  Suggestion: The following template files are used in GDP document processing exercises: Memo, Press Release, Purchase Order, Invoice, and all label template files. Use Windows Explorer to determine if all of these template files are installed with your word processor. If not, refer to your word processor's user's guide or online Help system to install the templates on your system.

- **A document or exercise does not get scored.**

  Explanation: The exercise is not supposed to be scored. Practice documents, warmups, new key presentations, and certain practice and skillbuilding and document processing exercises are not scored.

- **Scored copy contains numerous "<¶>" or "{¶}" marks.**

  Explanation: You did not follow the word wrap setting indicated in the exercise header at the top of the screen. A "<¶>" occurs in scored copy where word wrap is off and you fail to press **Enter** at the end of the line. A "{¶}" occurs in scored copy where word wrap is on and you mistakenly press **Enter** at the end of the line.

  Suggestion: Retype the exercise following the word wrap setting in the exercise header.

- **No sound plays at the end of timings or when the restart period is over in a timing.**

  Explanation: GDP uses the Default Sound to signal the end of a timing and the end of the restart period. Your computer either has <none> (no audible sound) assigned to the Default Sound, or it has speakers attached to the computer but not turned on.

  Suggestion: First, check to make sure that the Default Sound in your Windows 95/98/NT Sounds control panel is assigned an audible sound such as ding, chimes, or chord. (If you are not familiar with the Sounds control panel, refer to your Windows 95/98/NT user's guide.) Also make sure that your speakers (if any are attached to your computer) are turned on and work.

Appendix B: Error Marking and Speed Calculation

Error Marking

Errors in scored copy are marked as follows:

- <u>**Underlined red**</u>: all incorrect words.
- **<green in angle brackets>**: all omitted words, tabs (designated as <[T]>), and hard returns (designated as <¶>).
- **{Blue in braces}**: incorrectly inserted words, tabs (designated as {[T]}), and hard returns (designated as {¶}).

Examples:

Incorrect word	You <u>**cane**</u> go.
Omitted word	You **<can>** go.
Inserted word	You **{perhaps}** can go.
Inserted Tab	**{[T]}**You can go.
Omitted tab	**<[T]>**You can go.
Inserted hard return	You can go.**{¶}**
Omitted hard return	You can go.**<¶>**

Error Scores The most widely used rules for determining the error score on a timing are the International Typewriting Contest Rules. According to these rules, every actual word that differs from the original source copy counts as 1 error. The determination of errors by GDP is based on these rules.

Speed (WAM) Calculation

In all but numeric keypad exercises, GDP calculates, displays, and records the student's speed as wam—that is, as words a minute. A word equals 5 keystrokes (letters, spaces, tabs, hard returns, etc.). Like all other scores, each wam score is based on the copy in the book: incorrectly added strokes are not counted; similarly, incorrectly omitted strokes are not subtracted.

The words-a-minute (wam) speed is based on the following formulas.

- 12-second timings: Each letter or space counts as 1 wam.
- 30-second timings: Every 5 keystrokes (letters, spaces, tabs, and hard returns) count as 2 wam.
- Minute timings: The total number of 5-letter words is divided by the number of minutes in the timing.

25 words ÷ 1 minute = 25 wam

50 words ÷ 2 minutes = 25 wam

75 words ÷ 3 minutes = 25 wam

125 words ÷ 5 minutes = 25 wam

Note: Speed in numeric keypad exercises is reported in seconds, corresponding to the number of seconds it takes the student to complete the exercise. For example, S 193 indicates that it took the student 193 seconds to complete the exercise.

Index

K

L

M

N

O

P

R

S

T

U

V

W

P/N G05271.10

Glencoe/McGraw-Hill

A Division of The McGraw-Hill Companies